Getting Started With Google Sheets

A PRACTICAL GUIDE TO CLOUD-BASED SPREADSHEETS

Scott La Counte

ANAHEIM, CALIFORNIA

www.RidiculouslySimpleBooks.com

Copyright © 2019 by Scott La Counte.

All rights reserved. No part of this publication may be reproduced, distributed or transmitted in any form or by any means, including photocopying, recording, or other electronic or mechanical methods, without the prior written permission of the publisher, except in the case of brief quotations embodied in critical reviews and certain other noncommercial uses permitted by copyright law.

Limited Liability / Disclaimer of Warranty. While best efforts have been used in preparing this book, the author and publishers make no representations or warranties of any kind and assume no liabilities of any kind with respect to accuracy or completeness of the content and specifically the author nor publisher shall be held liable or responsible to any person or entity with respect to any loss or incidental r consequential damages caused or alleged to have been caused, directly, or indirectly without limitations, by the information or programs contained herein. Furthermore, readers should be aware that the Internet sites listed in this work may have changed or disappeared. This work is sold with the understanding that the advice inside may not be suitable in every situation.

Trademarks. Where trademarks are used in this book this infers no endorsement or any affiliation with this book. Any trademarks (including, but not limiting to, screenshots) used in this book are solely used for editorial and educational purposes.

Table of Contents

Google Sheets Crash Course *6*
    What is Google Sheets, Anyway? 6
    Excel vs. Google Sheets: What's Right For Me? 7
    The Google Sheets Crash Course 9

Getting Started With Google Sheets *13*
    Creating Your First Sheet 14
    Opening A Saved Document 16
    The Basics 17

Beyond the Basics *21*
    Creating a Chart 21
    Functionally Yours 28
    So Many Functions…That I Don't Want 31

Sharing is Caring *33*
    Sharing Your Sheet 33
    Editing and Collaborating With Others 38
    Protect a Spreadsheet 43
    Data Validation 43

This and That *47*

Survey's Into Data 47
This and That.. 54
Appendix: Keyboard Shortcuts............................... 63
About the Author 66

Disclaimer: Please note, while every effort has been made to ensure accuracy, this book is not endorsed by Alphabet, Inc. and should be considered unofficial.

[1]

Google Sheets Crash Course

This chapter will cover:
- What is Sheets?
- Should you still use Excel?
- The Google Sheets crash course

What is Google Sheets, Anyway?

For 30-some-odd years, the world of spreadsheets has been ruled by one king: Microsoft Excel. Sure, there were far away challengers that tried to overtake the beast—I'm looking at you, Lotus 1-2-

3—but none have come close to dethroning the powerful tool...until Google Sheets.

So what is Google Sheets? It's a cloud-based spreadsheet. Think Excel, but online. "But Excel is online," you say. Yes! But Google was there first, and really has the advantage over Excel in this arena. It's quicker and easier to use for collaboration.

Google Sheets is also free; Excel has monthly/yearly subscriptions.

Excel vs. Google Sheets: What's Right For Me?

If you are judging Google Sheets by mere looks, you might think it was a clone. It has tabs, it has cells, and, heck, even the formulas are largely the same!

So what is the difference?!

Let's go with the obvious one. As of this writing, you can add 5,000,000 cells to Google Sheets; Microsoft Excel? 17,179,869,184 cells.

How embarrassing, right? How on Earth can you get anything done with only 5,000,000 cells!

Kidding aside, that number does tell you one thing: Excel is the best software for large corporations managing budgets spanning dozens of years. But for the rest of us, that number really doesn't matter. A spreadsheet with 5,000,000 cells is plenty. The moment you get to cell 5,000,001 you have hopefully made it in the world and have sold your business. You now live on a private island where you ride llamas bareback on the beach. Why llamas? Because you are ridiculously wealthy and horses just seem too middleclass.

There is one other thing that's telling about that number, however. It's speed.

What do I mean by that? The reason Google limits cells is because in a cloud-based environment, the more cells you add, the slower it gets. Excel can afford crazy amounts of cells because it's locally installed. As long as you have a good computer with plenty of memory, you can have a nearly endless number of cells and not have to worry about things slowing down.

Again, most of us probably don't care about speed. We're working with smaller spreadsheets and never notice lags. But, and it's a big but, things do slow down when you start working with thousands of cells in Google, and that can be problematic for productivity.

The biggest reason people are switching to Google Sheets, however, is collaboration. Google is king when it comes to collaboration. If you are working on a budget with a group of people, then Google is hands down the way to go.

The Google Sheets Crash Course

The first three buttons are pretty straightforward: undo, redo what you have typed and print. The last one is the format painter; this lets you copy the style of one cell into another cell. To use it, click the cell you want to copy, select the format painter, and then click the cell you want to put the style in.

By default, a spreadsheet is viewed at 100%; if you are working with a larger sheet and want to see more cells on your screen, you can use this to zoom out—or also to zoom in and see less cells on your screen.

The next five options tell the cell what the content is. $ turns it into currency; % turns it into a percentage; the next two move the decimals forward and backward; and finally, the 123 gives you additional options to telling the cell what it is—plain text, a scientific formula, a date, etc. This is also useful if you have a number, but you want Google to treat it like plain text.

$$\$ \quad \% \quad .0 \quad .00 \quad 123 \blacktriangledown$$

If you have used any kind of productivity software, then you should know the next two options; if you've been under a rock: this is the font and font size.

$$\text{Arial} \blacktriangledown \quad 10 \blacktriangledown$$

Next to the font is the font formatter; here you can bold, italicize, strikethrough (i.e. put a line through the middle of the text), or change the number.

$$B \quad I \quad S \quad \underline{A}$$

The next set of options is for the cell style; you can change the fill color, the cell border, and merge cells. To merge cells, highlight the cells you want to merge and then click this option.

Justification and placement are managed in the next four options. Here you can center/right/left align, move the content to the bottom/middle/top of the cell, wrap the text (by default text will just spill over into the next cell unless you resize the cell; this option tells it to make the text go to the next line, sort of like hitting the enter key, since the enter/return key doesn't work in Sheets); and finally rotate text, which also lets you change the direction of the text.

The last set of options is to insert things into a cell. You can insert a link, comment, chart, filter, or function.

On the far side, is an up arrow. This just hides or unhides the toolbar.

^

[2]
Getting Started With Google Sheets

This chapter will cover:
- Your first Sheet
- Opening saved documents
- The basics

Okay, so how exactly do you use Google Sheets? Like everything else in the Google Suite family! The beauty of Google is once you learn one, learning others is pretty easy.

Here's a refresher: type in drive.google.com.

Once you have your Google account (hopefully you do by now), then you are all set. Repeat the step above and the browser Window should look more like the below.

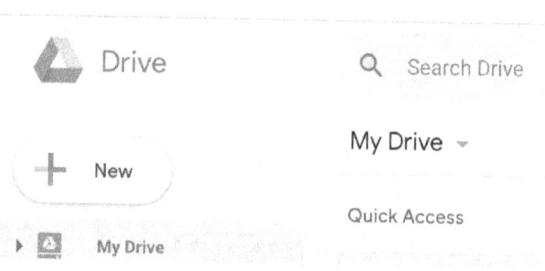

Creating Your First Sheet

Now that you have your account, let's create a document. Click on the "New" button and then hover over Google Sheets; there are two options: "Blank document" and "From a template." For now, select "From a template." I'll cover templates a little bit later.

At this point, you'll be taken to Google's Sheets editor. This is where you do the actual work. Everything is designed to function just like Excel or Numbers.

Have a look in the upper left-hand corner of your Google Sheets. You'll see a text field that says "Untitled Document." Click on that.

You will now be prompted with a box asking you to rename the document. I chose "My Glorious Google Sheet!," but you can type anything you want. When you finish, hit the enter key.

Once you do that, the top bar will change, reflecting the new name you've chosen:

My Glorious Google Sheet! in My Drive
File   Edit   View   Insert   Format   Data   Tools   Add-ons   Help   All changes saved in Drive

Do you see the text on the right where it says, "All changes saved"? That's another awesome thing about Google Sheets:

All changes saved in Drive

In a stroke of pure brilliance, the folks at Google have decided to completely automate document saves. As you write, Google saves your project and tells you when it last did this. If you want, you can go ahead and save, but it's practically unnecessary. Google Sheets saves after you enter every new word.

Opening A Saved Document

Don't worry about accidentally closing your tab. When you open it back up, Google will take you right back to your list of documents. You should see your document at the top of that list in "Quick Access."

If you are just getting started, it will also be the only sheet you see, and you can access it below the quick access

List view looks like the above—it gives the name, who the owner is, and the time it was edited. Grid view is more of a thumbnail preview of the Sheet.

Notice how "author" and "time lasted edited" is gone?

What's better? It's a preference, but if you are working with dozens of files, then Grid view probably will not be ideal unless you need to see previews.

To toggle between the two, click these icons in the upper corner:

List is the horizontal lines, and grid is the six square boxes.

The most recently viewed and edited files gets the top spot.

When you double-click on the Sheet or document you want, it'll open right up in the browser, and we can get back to writing. It's just like opening up an Excel or Numbers document on your home computer.

The Basics

Now that we've gotten our quick crash course, let's add some numbers and see how this thing works.

I'll start by adding some years; like any good spreadsheet software, Google is pretty good at guessing. If there's a pattern, then you can autofill the cells. In the example below, I've added two years: 1900 and 1901. When I highlight those two cells, there's a tiny blue box:

	A
1	Year
2	1900
3	1901

If I drag that blue box down, Google will correctly predict that I am putting years in and add one year per cell for as long as I drag:

	A
1	Year
2	1900
3	1901
4	1902
5	1903
6	1904
7	1905
8	1906
9	1907
10	1908
11	1909
12	1910
13	

For this example, I'm going to create another column that shows how many babies were born, then two fields to show the total babies and average babies born.

To get the total number, go to the cell and type "=sum(". Google will probably highlight what it thinks you want automatically, but if it doesn't, then just highlight the cells you want to add up and then hit Enter/Return:

Year	Babies Born
1900	33
1901	100
1902	4
1903	22
1904	21
1905	99
1906	73
1907	9
1908	9
1909	60
1910	81

Babies Born	=SUM
Average	SUM(B2:B12)
	Suggested based on the data

The same method is used for averages, but you type =average(instead of sum:

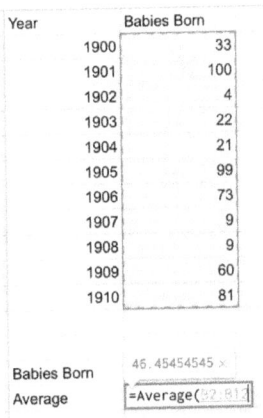

In seconds, we now know the number of babies born as well as the average for all years:

Year	Babies Born
1900	33
1901	100
1902	4
1903	22
1904	21
1905	99
1906	73
1907	9
1908	9
1909	60
1910	81
Babies Born	511
Average	46.45454545

Not happy with how it looks? You can apply basic formatting the same way you would in a Google Doc or Word Doc:

Year	Babies Born
1900	33
1901	100
1902	4
1903	22
1904	21
1905	
1906	73
1907	9
1908	9
1909	60
1910	81
Babies Born	412
Average	41.2

[3]
BEYOND THE BASICS

This chapter will cover:
- Creating charts
- Functions
- Scripts

Creating a Chart

People are visual. Numbers aren't very sexy. You need visuals to make them pop.

Before we go deeper into the fun world of functions, let's take the fun out of functions and do something fun: a chart.

I'll take the example above and create a chart that shows the babies born per year a little more visually.

To get started, I'll highlight what I want to show; in my example, only the top portion—the chart doesn't need to show the totals or averages:

	A	B
1	Year	Babies Born
2	1900	33
3	1901	100
4	1902	4
5	1903	22
6	1904	21
7	1905	99
8	1906	73
9	1907	9
10	1908	9
11	1909	60
12	1910	81
13		
14		
15	Babies Born	511
16	Average	46.45454545

Next, go to the toolbar and click the chart icon:

And just like that, we have a pretty line graph that represents our data:

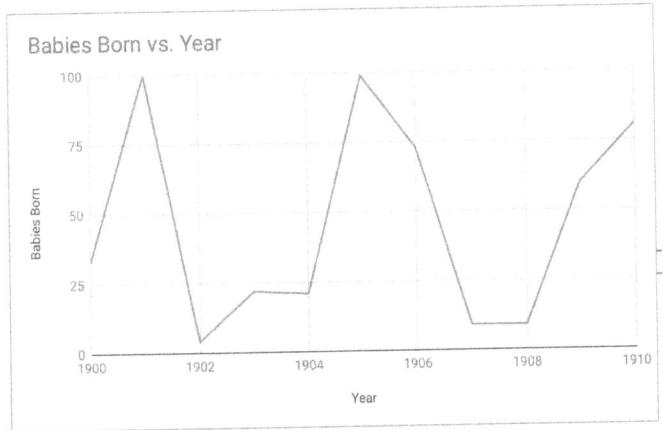

I know, I know...you're sitting there thinking: Lines! I hate lines!

Don't fret! You use the chart editor that opens a chart library to create dozens of other charts:

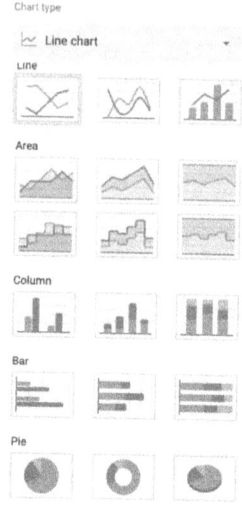

If you got so excited when the chart came up on your screen that you accidentally closed the chart editor, then just double click the chart and it will open back up:

You can use this editor to change the range (you add some more rows, for example, and want them represented) or reverse the data shown—you want to show the years on the lines, not the number of babies born.

Google has its own idea of what is pretty. It's probably different from yours. You don't want a blue line! You want a red line! You hate the black text! You want green! If there's one thing

Spreadsheet people are known for, it's their incredible talent for making numbers look sexy. Don't worry! You can customize almost everything here.

If you need to bring sexy back to your chart, then just go into your editor and select "Customize" right next to "Setup."

Setup   Customize

From here you can go section-to-section and change colors, fonts, and more:

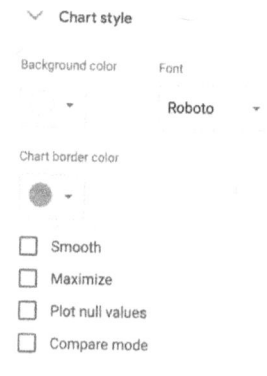

You can also change gridlines around on the bottom:

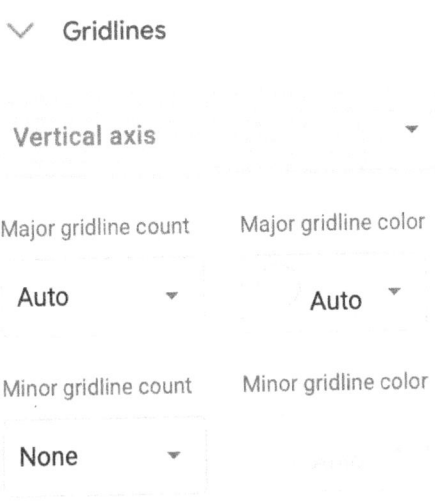

By default, Google will just stick the chart inconveniently over your data. If you click on it, you'll see a bunch of little blue boxes. That means you can either resize it (click on one and drag in/out to make it larger/smaller) or move it:

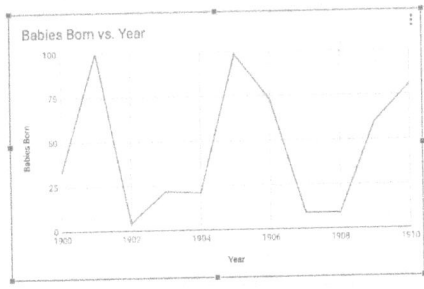

You'll also notice three little boxes in the upper right corner of the chart. That's your chart menu. Click that and you'll see several options:

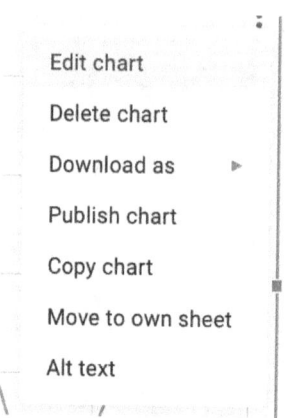

Download as is helpful if you want to insert it into emails as attachments or presentations. You can download it as an image or PDF.

You can also copy and paste the chart into other Google app—like Google Slides or Google Docs. Just click it and do CTRL+C on your keyboard to copy it, and CTRL+V to paste it.

Functionally Yours

Now that we had some fun, let's get serious and learn about functions.

What is a function exactly? Well, we already learned about two: Sum and Average. Functions are the formulas you put into cells to tell Google to calculate an equation.

There are a lot of functions. Go to your toolbar and click the function key, and you can see what I mean!

The main ones you use will be right at the top, which is helpful; below that, Google has categorized additional ones.

Because this book is meant to get you started quickly and not teach you all the features that you will never use, I won't cover every single function here. The goal is to show you how they work, so if there's one not covered here that you want to use, you'll know how.

I recommend you spend a few minutes looking at the list above and see if there's something that would be useful to what you are doing. There are hundreds of functions.

To use any of the functions in this list, go to the cell you want to show the equation in, and then click the function option and select the one you want to do; from here, select your data range. Once it's selected, hit return/enter.

If you decide later that you need to edit the function, go to the upper left corner—just under the tool bar. See the fx? When you select a cell with a function, it will show up here. Click in there, and then update the range that you want.

That's also the same place you go to edit anything in a cell—function or no function.

So Many Functions...That I Don't Want

Google Sheets has a lot of functions. It's overwhelming, but it doesn't have everything. If you become a power spreadsheets user, you might find it would be helpful to do something that there is no function for.

That doesn't mean you can't do it. It's just a little more involved. There are many more things you can do by creating a script. Scripts let you basically program your own function.

Scripts can be found by going to Tools > Scripts Editor.

This is going to launch a separate Google app for creating a script:

Below is an example of what a script might look like:

```
var ss = SpreadsheetApp.getActiveSpreadsheet();
var sheet = ss.getSheets()[0];

// The size of the two-dimensional array must match the size of
var values = [
    [ "2.000", "1,000,000", "$2.99" ]
];

var range = sheet.getRange("B2:D2");
range.setValues(values);
```

Once you have your script written, go to Publish > Deploy as Sheets add-on:

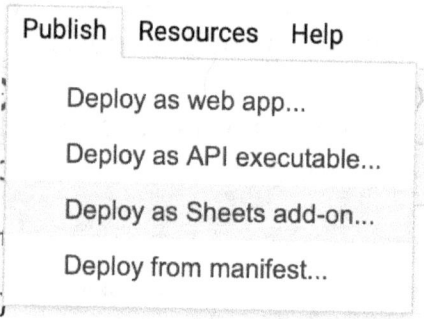

The topic of scripts is much too complicated for this book, but there are plenty of resources both in the Scripts app and online if this is an arena you'd like to dig deeper into later.

[4]
SHARING IS CARING

This chapter will cover:
- Sharing your sheet
- Editing and collaborating sheets
- Protecting sheets
- Data validation

Sharing Your Sheet

Now that you know your way around, you're ready for feedback from others.

If you know how to share a Google Doc, then you are in luck! Sharing Sheets is the same. Need a refresher?

Look up in the upper right corner. See the blue button that says Share? Click on that. It's going to open up several different sharing options.

When you click on that, a share box opens up, and you get a bunch of different options.

There's a few ways to share it:
1. Type their email address and let Google do the rest.
2. Manually (covered below).

When you email someone, you can also manage exactly what they can do. Click that little pencil icon. By default, it will say they can edit the doc. You can change it so they can only comment on the doc, or they can only view the doc:

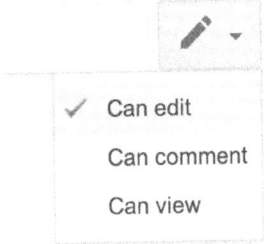

You can also hit advance at the bottom of the share menu, and have a few more features—such as disabling print:

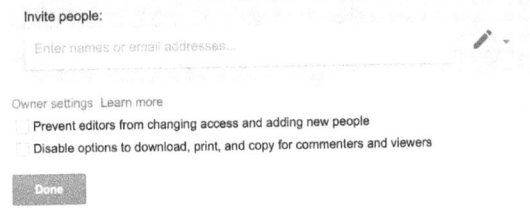

But let's say you don't want to email the first man. Let's say you just want to give him a link—that way he doesn't need to use his Google account to open it. To do that, follow the steps above, but in the upper corner of the box, click "Get shareable link."

Get shareable link

Once you click that, it will give you a sharable link—it even copies the link so if you hit CTRL-V (or right-click paste) you can paste that link anywhere you want.

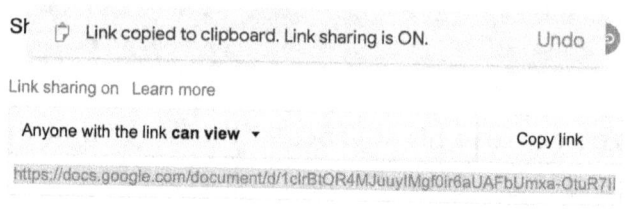

If you click on can view, it will give you a drop-down menu with more features. It looks sort of like the other drop-down menu above, but there's an option that says "more."

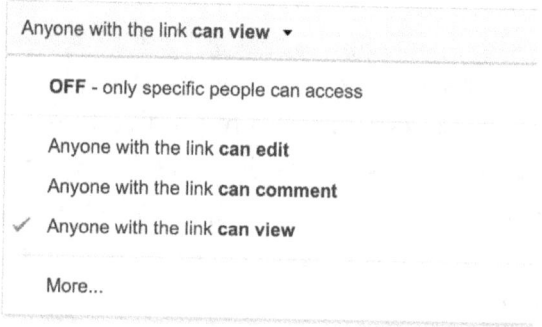

When you click on "More," it gives you a few extra features—such as making the document public in search engines so anyone can find it.

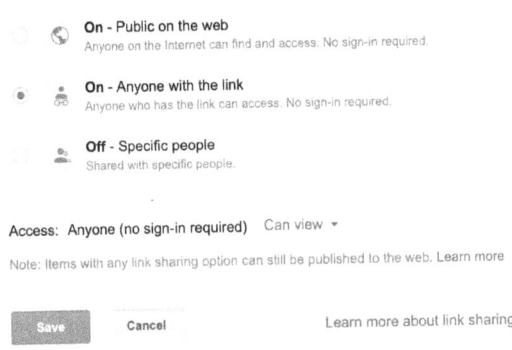

You can turn sharing off at any time, by hitting the "Share" button; once it's turned off, anyone who goes to that link—even if they've been there before—won't be able to see it. If you've emailed a person, they are still a viewer until you remove them.

If you have a person who really hates Google Sheets and refuses to view your document in anything but Word, Google Docs allows you to export your work to a Excel Document so you don't have to do all of the copying and font processing yourself. Just click on file --> download as --> Excel; there's a whole host of other exports here as well.

Editing and Collaborating With Others

The easiest way to make comments in a spreadsheet is to right-click and select Comment.

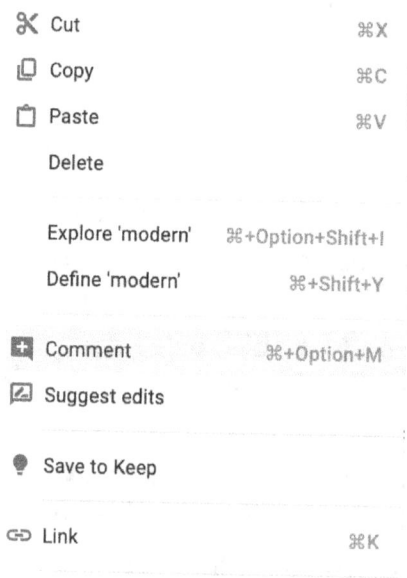

You can also get this, by selecting Insert on the toolbar, and Comment.

Either of these will bring up the comment box. Add your comment, and select the blue comment box when you are ready to post it. When you add a comment (or make a change), it's in real-time; that means if the person who is collaborating with you has the document open, they can actually watch you make the edits and add the comments.

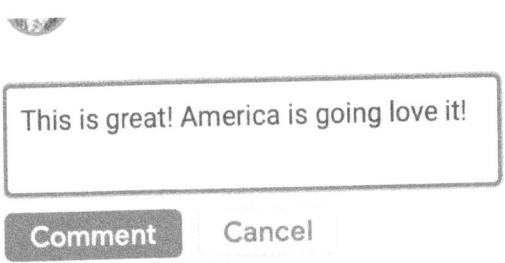

If you have multiple people working on the doc, you can type "@" and see a list of people you can mention; if you mention them, Google will notify them so they can add a reply to your comment.

Once the comments in, it will show up on the side of Google Sheets.

ph

our

This is

You can delete or edit the comment, by click on those three little dots on the side of the box.

Edit

Delete

Link to this comment...

The person on the other end will be able to resolve the comment (that makes it disappear, but they can undo it)

Or they can reply to it.

To see all the versions of a document, go to file and see versions.

Version history ▶	Name current version	
Rename	See version history	⌘+Option+Shift+H

If there's going to be a lot of versions, then one suggestion is to name each one—which you can do here.

When you click See version history, you'll get a list of all the versions. Clicking on anyone will bring up that version. You can view it, or even restore it.

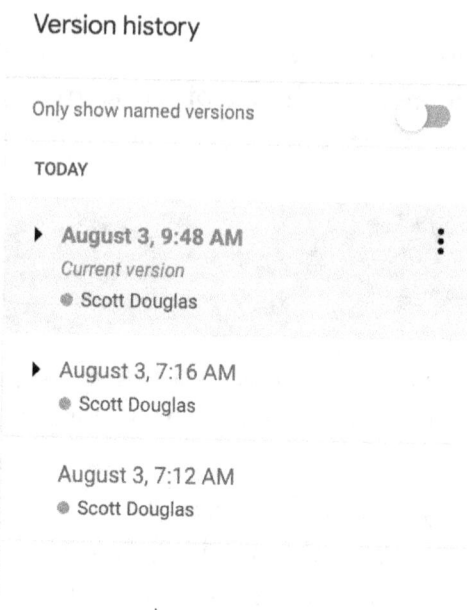

To get back to the document, just hit the back button in the menu (not the browser back button).

← Today, 9:48 AM

Protect a Spreadsheet

Google Sheets has an extra layer of protection not seen in Google Docs. To apply it, go to Tools > Protect Sheet.

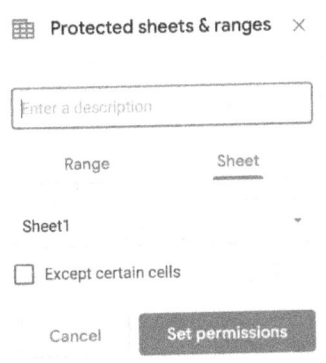

From here you can do several things:

Give it a description – Why does it need a description? Because you can create several difference protections.

Select the range.

Set permissions – you can, for example, give one person the ability to make changes and another the ability only to see it.

Data Validation

Let's say you give someone permission to edit the sheet and they add in something wrong; that error messes up the entire spreadsheet! Now what? Spent hours trying to figure out the mess they made, right?

Sure, why not! But why don't we make sure they don't make that mess to begin with!

Data validation let's you add in rules so people can't add in things incorrectly. For example, let's say someone doesn't know the answer so they just put in "?" or "N/A." You can set up a rule that forces them only to use a number.

To add one in, highlight the cells you want to apply it to and then go to Data > Data validation. This brings up the option box.

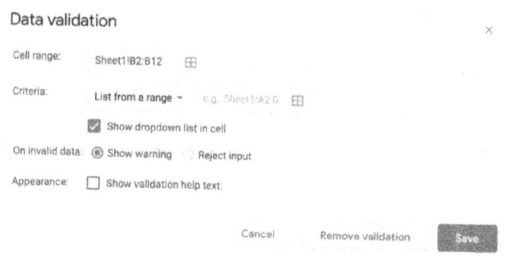

From here you need to set your rule (or criteria).

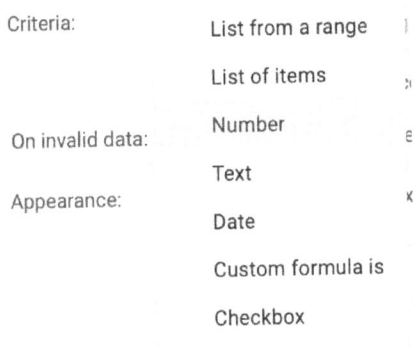

My rule is the data here needs to be a number between 0 and 101. If you want to get really fancy, you can add in a custom formula.

Next, you need to say what happens if they break the rule. Do you want to outright reject it or just give them a warning. In my case, I'm all about rejection. But I'm a nice guy too, so I'm going to tell them why I'm rejecting them.

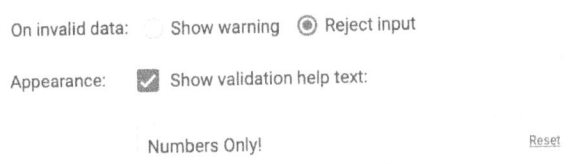

Now if someone tries to add anything but a number, then tell get this message.

There was a problem

Numbers Only!

OK

[5]
THIS AND THAT

This chapter will cover:
- Surveys
- Google Sheets menus

Survey's Into Data

One area Google Sheets has Excel and other programs beat is it's survey integration.

Using Google Forms to create a survey, you can have all the answers go right into a Google Sheet so you can collate your results.

To get started go to Insert > Forms.

This is going to launch a separate tab with the Google Forms application.

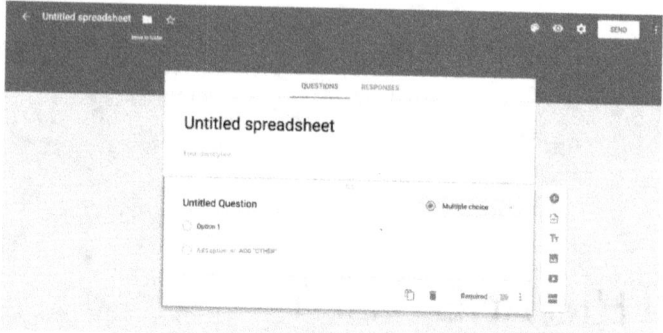

I'm going to make this survey simple, but if you want to jazz it up, there's all kinds of options for adding photos and changing styles around. Use the menu on the right side for those options.

For my survey, I'm going to make it a drop-down survey. You can change the question type by selecting the drop down to the right side of the question name; you can have as many types as you want in the survey—for example, question one could be multiple choice and question two could be a drop down.

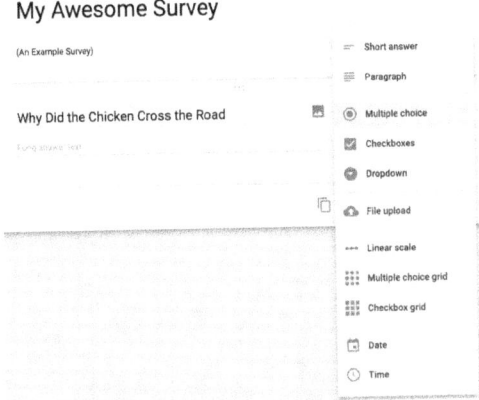

This changes our answers to editable fields. Right now, it has room for two questions. As soon as I stop typing in the second answer, a slot will be added for a third question.

More answer slots are added with each question.

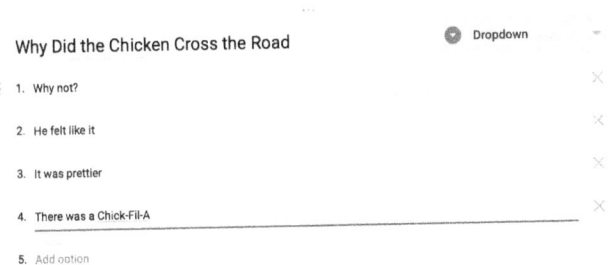

When you are done, click the "Send Form" button in the upper right corner:

I don't want to send the form to anyone—I want it to be a link. So, I'm going to click the link icon next to the email one (it's the middle one).

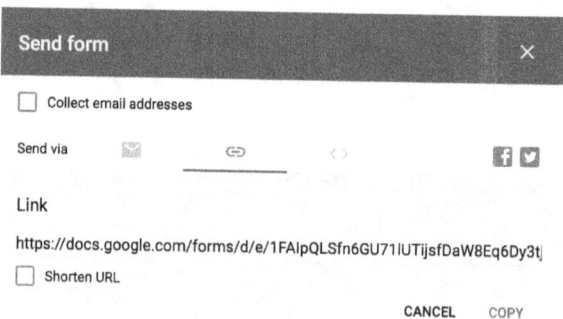

When someone goes to my survey, it will look a little bit different from the one that was in the editor because all the menu fields are gone.

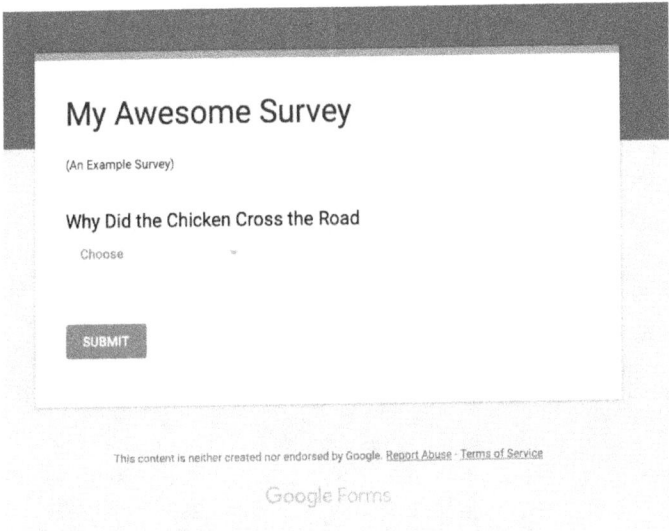

Once they click submit, they'll see a confirmation. You can make this a custom confirmation or use the default Google one.

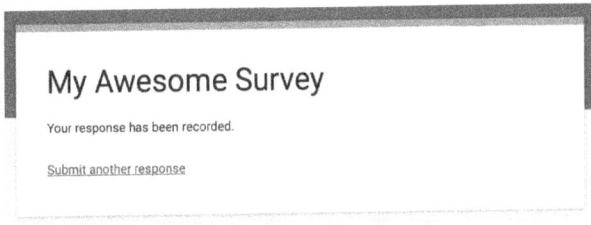

Now that you have a response, go back to your Sheet and you'll see a new tab has been added on the bottom of the sheet for form responses.

Click that and you can see what the person answered.

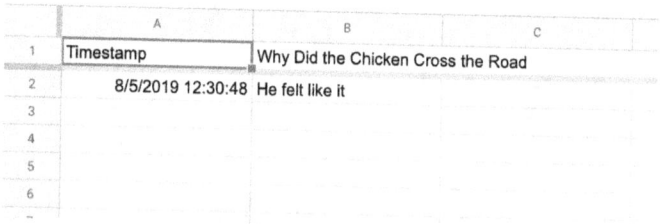

If you need to make changes to it, just go to Form from your menu bar.

Form   Add-ons   Help   All changes :

Edit form

Send form

Go to live form

Embed form in a webpage

Show summary of responses

Unlink form

If you have multiple forms, then this option will not show on your menu bar unless you are inside that form tab. So if you don't see the option, then click the tab for the Form responses and then it will appear in the menu.

If you decide to delete the form, it's a little different from a normal tab. A normal tab, you right-click on the tab and hit delete, it will tell you that you can't. You have to unlink it first. How? Easy!

Right-click on the form tab you want to unlink and select Unlink form.

Unlink form

Move right

Move left

Form Responses 1

Once it's unlinked, you'll be able to delete it, by right-clicking and selecting delete.

This and That

By now, you should be have a really good idea how Google Sheets work. Before leaving you, I'll cover a few more features that you should know about.

By default, Google will base the Sheet on your Google Account; if your Google Account thinks you live in Spain, then that's how the Sheet is set up.

You can change this by going to File > Spreadsheet settings.

Spreadsheet settings

This is helpful if you, for example, live in the United States, but happen to be working on a

Sheet for someone who lives in the UK. You can change the settings, so it shows as pounds instead of dollars.

When you start working on large documents, it gets difficult to find things. Imagine you have 100,000 cells and you have to find the one with the number "12a?b44." Good luck with that! Fortunately for you, there's something called "Find and Replace" under the Edit menu.

Not only does it find the cell you are looking for, but it let's you replace it with something else. For example, I can tell it to find every example of "California" and replace it with "CA."

Another handy feature if you have lots of rows is the freeze option. That's under View > Freeze.

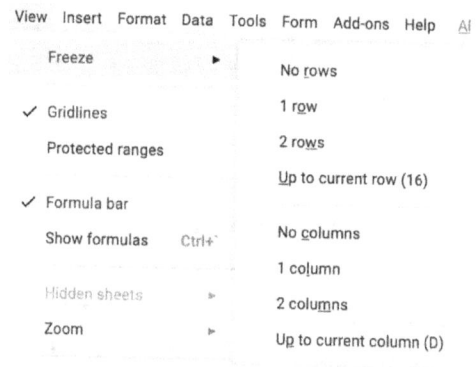

What exactly is freeze? Typically, you have a top row that is sort of like a menu. It tells the view what is in each column. And then you have the first column that has something else descriptive—such as dates. Now imagine you have 10,000 rows. You're on row 2079, column AA. You can't remember what that row stands for. If you had freeze row enabled, then that top menu (or side column) would be frozen, so no matter where you are, you always see it.

If you are editing a lot of formulas, go to View and check off "Show formulas." This will show you the formula instead of the answer. It's helpful for editing formulas.

✓ Formula bar

✓ Show formulas   Ctrl+`

If you are in the middle of a large sheet and need to add in a row in the middle, then select the row you want to add it to, then go to Insert > and select Row above, Row below, or anywhere else you want it.

Insert Format Data Tools For

Row **above**

Row **below**

Column **left**

Column **right**

Cells and shift **down**

Cells and shift **right**

Insert > Checkbox is useful if you have people viewing it and you want them to confirm that they see something.

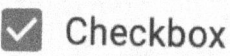 Checkbox

If you want to add a new tab to the bottom of your sheet, you can either click the + in the lower left corner of the sheet, or go to Insert > New sheet. To delete the sheet, right-click the tab and select delete.

| New sheet | Shift+F11 |

You learned earlier about setting rules to a Sheet with data validation. You can do something similar with format. This is found in Format > Conditional formatting.

Conditional formatting

With conditional formatting, you can, for example, tell the sheet if the cell is empty, it's green, but if it has content, then it's blue. You can do it for run cell, or highlight multiple cells to do it for several.

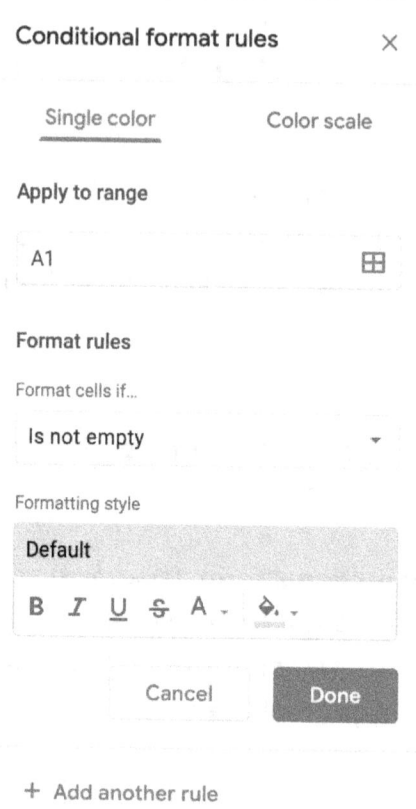

If you are working with a large sheet, and want to make sure there's no duplicate content, then highlight the range, then select Data > Remove duplicates. This will go through the range and remove anything that's the same.

Remove duplicates

Macros are a bit complex, they help you create sequences to automate certain tasks. I won't cover them here, but if you want to use them, it's under Tools > Macro.

Also under tools is Notification rules.

Notification rules

This is what you will use if you want to be notification when someone edits your document, or adds something to your survey. You can either be emailed immediately or once a day.

Set notification rules   Help ×

Notify me at roboscott@gmail.com when...
 ◯ Any changes are made
 ◯ A user submits a form

Notify me with...
 ◯ Email - daily digest
 ◯ Email - right away

                Cancel   Save

There's still a lot to learn, but I hope you now have the understanding and using Sheets comfortably.

If you find yourself copying a lot of formulas and getting errors, try pasting only the values. That means it will only copy the number and not the actual formula. You can do this by pressing CTRL+Shift+V, or by going to Edit > Paste special.

APPENDIX: KEYBOARD SHORTCUTS

You can see all the keyboard shortcuts in Google Sheets by selecting Help > Keyboard shortcuts.

For your reference, below are some of the most common ones you'll use.

Common actions

Select column	Ctrl + Space
Select row	Shift + Space
Select all	Ctrl + a
Undo	Ctrl + z
Redo	Ctrl + y
Find	Ctrl + f
Find and replace	Ctrl + h

Fill range	Ctrl + Enter
Fill down	Ctrl + d
Fill right	Ctrl + r
Copy	Ctrl + c
Cut	Ctrl + x
Paste	Ctrl + v
Paste values only	Ctrl + Shift + v

Format cells

Bold	Ctrl + b
Underline	Ctrl + u
Italic	Ctrl + i
Strikethrough	Alt + Shift + 5
Center align	Ctrl + Shift + e
Left align	Ctrl + Shift + l
Right align	Ctrl + Shift + r
Apply top border	Alt + Shift + 1
Apply right border	Alt + Shift + 2
Apply bottom border	Alt + Shift + 3
Apply left border	Alt + Shift + 4
Remove borders	Alt + Shift + 6
Apply outer border	Alt + Shift + 7
Insert link	Ctrl + k
Insert time	Ctrl + Shift + ;
Insert date	Ctrl + ;
Insert date and time	Ctrl + Alt + Shift + ;
Format as decimal	Ctrl + Shift + 1
Format as time	Ctrl + Shift + 2
Format as date	Ctrl + Shift + 3
Format as currency	Ctrl + Shift + 4
Format as percentage	Ctrl + Shift + 5
Format as exponent	Ctrl + Shift + 6
Clear formatting	Ctrl + \

Use formulas

Show all formulas	Ctrl + ~
Insert array formula	Ctrl + Shift + Enter
Collapse an expanded array formula	Ctrl + e
Show/hide formula help *(when entering a formula)*	Shift + F1
Full/compact formula help *(when entering a formula)*	F1
Absolute/relative references *(when entering a formula)*	F4
Toggle formula result previews *(when entering a formula)*	F9
Resize formula bar *(move up or down)*	Ctrl + Up / Ctrl + Down

ABOUT THE AUTHOR

Scott La Counte is a librarian and writer. His first book, *Queit, Please: Dispatches from a Public Librarian* (Da Capo 2008) was the editor's choice for the Chicago Tribune and a Discovery title for the Los Angeles Times; in 2011, he published the YA book The N00b Warriors, which became a #1 Amazon bestseller; his most recent book is *#OrganicJesus: Finding Your Way to an Unprocessed, GMO-Free Christianity* (Kregel 2016).

He has written dozens of best-selling how-to guides on tech products.

You can connect with him at ScottDouglas.org.